Saved by the
FLAME OF LOVE

Saved by the
FLAME OF LOVE

Alpha and Omega

Deacon Norman Alexander

www.DeaconNormanAlexander.com

SAVED BY THE FLAME OF LOVE
Deacon Norman Alexander

Copyright 2020, Deacon Norman Alexander

No part of this book may be reproduced, stored in a retrieval system, or transmitted by any means, electronic, mechanical, photocopying, recording, or otherwise, without written permission from the author.

Editor: Sam Severn
Graphic Designer: Debbi Stocco, MyBookDesigner.com

Scripture quotations are from the New American Bible and the Douay Rheims Bible.

paperback ISBN 13: 978-0-9912011-5-0
hardback ISBN 13: 978-0-9912011-6-7
ebook ISBN 13: 978-0-578-6561-1-3

For information regarding permission, write to:
Permissions Department
6102 Explorer Ave
Bartlett, TN 38134

Or contact via website:
www.deaconnormanalexander.com

Table of Contents

PART I—FROM BEGINNING TO PENTECOST

Introduction: The Great Miracle 9
   WATER FOR THE DESTRUCTION OF FLESH 11
   FIRE FOR THE SALVATION OF SOULS 11

Chapter I: The Flood 13
   NOAH'S ARK—EIGHT INDIVIDUALS REPLENISHED THE EARTH 13

Chapter II: Fire and Brimstone 17
   LOT'S HOME—FOUR INDIVIDUALS PRESERVED THEIR LINEAGE 17

Chapter III: The Red Sea 23
   MOSES AND THE ISRAELITES CROSSED THE RED SEA 23

Chapter IV: Mount Sinai 25
   MOSES AND THE LEVITES REDEEMED THE FIRSTBORN 25

Chapter V: The Jordan River 31
   JOSHUA AND THE ISRAELITES CROSSED THE JORDAN RIVER 31

Chapter VI: The Upper Room 39
   PETER AND THE ISRAELITES SENT FROM THE UPPER ROOM 39

PART II—FROM PENTECOST TO BEGINNING

Chapter VII: House of the Carmelite Fathers 45
   I INVITE THOSE LIVING IN THE HOUSE OF THE CARMELITE FATHERS—THE UPPER ROOM 45

Chapter VIII: A New Instrument 53
   I WOULD LIKE TO PLACE IN YOUR HANDS A NEW INSTRUMENT—CROSSING THE JORDAN 53

Chapter IX: From Mount Carmel 61
   THE FLAME OF LOVE MUST GO FORTH FROM THE CARMEL—
   MOUNT SINAI 61
   CHART 1—FROM THE CARMEL 65
   CHART 2—PENTECOSTAL EXPERIENCE 66
   CHART 3—THE NEW PENTECOSTAL EXPERIENCE 67

Chapter X: Other Side of the Ocean 71
   MY FLAME OF LOVE MUST BE CARRIED ACROSS TO THE OTHER
   SIDE OF THE OCEAN—THE RED SEA 71

Chapter XI: Those Signed with the Cross 79
   ALL THE SOULS MARKED WITH THE SIGN OF THE BLESSED CROSS
   OF MY DIVINE SON—LOT AND FAMILY 79

Chapter XII: Even the Non-Baptized 85
   THE EFFUSION OF GRACES WILL ALSO REACH THE SOULS OF THE
   NON-BAPTIZED—THE FLOOD 85

PART I—FROM BEGINNING TO PENTECOST

Introduction

The Great Miracle

AT DIFFERENT TIMES IN HISTORY, humanity takes a path of self-destruction. It may be a small group, a large group or even the entire world, but at those times of self-destruction God comes to the rescue. The solution to such problems may not be easily understood. For instance, when God decides to wipe out an evil and perverse generation, we may look at this as total destruction rather than mercy. The reality is that God is always concerned with the salvation of souls. Once we understand this, it is easier to trust God, rather than judge Him.

The Flame of Love of the Immaculate Heart of Mary is known as the greatest gift to us since the Word became flesh. The Spiritual Diary of Elizabeth Kindelmann has several statements that articulate this message, signifying its importance. I love this expression: "There has never been a time of grace like this since the Word became flesh." It is understood among *Flame of Love* devotees that this flame will spread over the entire earth. The

Flame of Love is the great miracle that will blind Satan and save souls. We must never forget that we are fighting a war—a mysterious one at that, because God desires the salvation of every human soldier, on both sides of the battlefield.

The Blessed Mother told Elizabeth: *"Enter into battle, we will be the conquerors. My Flame of Love will blind Satan to the same extent that all of you spread it around the world. Just as the whole world knows my name, so I want the Flame of Love of my heart performing miracles in the depths of the hearts to also be known. There will be no need to investigate this miracle. All will feel its authenticity within their hearts. Whoever has felt it once will communicate it to others because my grace will be active in them. There is no need for authentication. I will authenticate it myself in every soul so that all recognize the effusion of grace of my Flame of Love."* (Spiritual Diary of Elizabeth Kindelmann, page 99.)

The urgency of this message makes clear that there is no time to waste. The fire of hatred in the world hurls high enough to cause Satan to believe he has victory. The Flame of Love will extinguish this fire of hatred, but we are expected to participate in this work of redemption. We have been given a great responsibility: the salvation of souls worldwide. Is there an ark large enough for everyone to fit into? Yes, the Flame of Love of the Immaculate Heart of Mary.

Jesus and the Blessed Virgin made reference to people and events in Sacred Scripture, and even referred to more current events. The Spiritual Diary appears as a most awesome and masterfully written work of art, yet the message itself is simple and clear. For those of us who have received the gift of the Flame of Love, but love to ponder the meaning and essence of great and wonderful mysteries, we have in our hands one of the greatest biblical commentaries ever written. The gift of the Flame of Love is meant for everyone living in these times, and everyone who welcomes it will be enlightened. The soft light of the Flame of Love will enlighten the minds and give warmth to the hearts of all who receive it.

During February of 2019, I published a title called, "Unity and the Flame of Love." It is a small book, whose contents stretch over a large span of salvation history—very large actually, from the beginning to present. This book is similar, because it is about the Alpha and the Omega, the beginning and the end, the first and the last.

WATER FOR THE DESTRUCTION OF FLESH

Jesus is the Alpha and the Omega, the beginning and the end. He told Elizabeth Kindelmann, *"The Flame of Love of my mother's heart is Noah's Ark."* The Catechism of the Catholic Church states that the flood prefigured baptism and Noah's ark prefigured the church. In Baptism, we enter the ark by becoming members of the Body of Christ. *"You were buried with Him in baptism, in which you were also raised with Him through faith in the power of God, who raised Him from the dead."* (Col 2:12) Thus Baptism is the first sacrament we receive making us citizens of the Kingdom of God.

FIRE FOR THE SALVATION OF SOULS

The Blessed Virgin said to Elizabeth, *"You have to seek a refuge for my Flame of Love, which is Jesus Christ Himself."* Pentecost was a baptism of the Holy Spirit and of fire, when the church was born out of the upper room, and the disciples were sent out as witnesses. In the sacrament of Confirmation, we are sent out to replenish the earth. Tongues of fire over the heads of the disciples portrayed the image of head and body going out together to set the earth on fire. The Flame of Love is like the first Pentecost—the difference being the fire is in the hearts of the disciples. The mission is the same: to set the earth on fire. The Divine Love will extinguish the fire of hatred.

Jesus is the Alpha and the Omega, the beginning and the end. Both the flood waters and the fire were meant to extend over the entire earth. The flood for the destruction of all flesh, and the fire for the salvation of souls. Although many will refuse to enter the ark, God desires that all are saved, and come to the knowledge of the truth.

Here are six historical accounts in the Bible that reveal a group being wiped out and another group being saved. Listed in chronological order, they are:

1. Water—Noah and the flood, which covered the entire earth.
2. Fire—Lot escaped the fire and brimstone that destroyed Sodom and Gomorrah.
3. Water—The Israelites passing through the Red Sea.
4. Fire—The fire which covered Mount Sinai.
5. Water—The Israelites crossing the Jordan River.
6. Fire—Tongues of fire in the upper room.

Chapter 1

The Flood

Noah's Ark—Eight Individuals Replenished the Earth

The story of Noah and the ark is one of the more popular biblical stories. It seems that most people are familiar with the idea of a great deluge that covered the whole earth. Not only do Jews and Christians have an account of a great flood, but other nations and peoples also have their version of a similar flood recorded in their historical archives.

The cause of the flood given to us in Sacred Scripture is that humanity had seemingly reached a point of no return. The degree of lawlessness and evil in the world was at an all-time high, and the Lord deemed it necessary to save humanity from total destruction by purging the earth and starting over. He said, *"Man is but flesh and every desire of his heart is but evil."* But Noah found favor with the Lord. He said to Noah, *"I have decided to put an end to all mortals on earth; the earth is full of lawlessness because of them. So I will destroy them and all life on earth."* (Genesis 6:13)

"Make for yourself an ark of gopherwood, put various compartments and cover it inside and out with pitch." And the Lord gave Noah all the instructions for building the ark: dimensions, provisions for daylight and every necessary detail. *"I, on my part, am about to bring the flood waters on the earth, to destroy everywhere all creatures in which there is the breath of life; everything on earth shall perish. But with you I will establish my covenant; you and your sons, your wife and your sons' wives shall go into the ark."* (Genesis 6:17-18) Noah followed the instructions of the Lord to also bring along creatures from every species on earth, and provisions for his family and all the creatures, in order to preserve them from extinction.

In the six hundredth year of Noah's life in the second month, on the seventeenth day of the month: it was on that day that
All the fountains of the great abyss
burst forth,
and the floodgates of the sky
were opened.
For forty days and forty nights heavy rain poured down on the earth. (Genesis 7:11-12)

Reference to the flood has been repeated in Sacred Scripture and in church history. The six and forty is a constant reminder of the destruction of the temple. From the time of the Crucifixion, the destruction of the temple has always been a reference to the sufferings of the members of Jesus' body, the church.

Listen to the words of Elizabeth Kindelmann: *"Doubts, similar to the ones I have just mentioned and exposed, arose in many diverse ways, stirred in my soul and struck me for years. They kept occurring even in my sixty-four years of life [in 1977].*

"The story of one of my most serious doubts and crises, with

respect to consequences, I reveal it with what follows:

"On one occasion, when these strong doubts came upon me, I once again sought peace of soul. To gain this peace, I decided to retract the words and the messages of the Lord Jesus and the Blessed Virgin before all those to whom I had given them. I acted on this decision. I went to twelve Hungarian priests and said to each one: 'Do not believe what I have told you because it all comes from me. They are lies I invented.' While crying and sobbing, I asked them for their absolution. They reacted in different ways and gave their opinion. I told them, without hiding anything, that my terrible torments were forcing me to retract." (Spiritual Diary of Elizabeth Kindelmann, page 289.)

The world, enslaved to the devil, because of the fear of death, has been redeemed by Jesus. But Jesus allowed the devil to torment Elizabeth Kindelmann. He tormented her to the point that she was willing to reject the messages of the Lord and the Blessed Virgin. She suffered this for our benefit. Her experience allows us to be enlightened by the Flame of Love of the need to be humble and merciful, as Jesus and Mary are. Elizabeth Kindelmann was allowed to suffer the same fate as our first mother, Eve. The same type of torments plagued Martin Luther. Eve no longer believed what was revealed to her through Adam, and Martin Luther no longer believed in the teaching authority of the Roman Catholic Church.

All of this is about the way to eternal life. Satan's torments can cause a person to lose faith and reject the way that was pointed out to them, along with legitimate teaching authority. The devil torments people by placing doubt in their mind, to make them give up the truth—because the truth is the way to eternal life. If one gives up the truth to end the suffering and restore peace of soul, that sheep will stray from the flock. Jesus was taunted and tormented that way during his Passion. Yet, he remained faithful to the truth, because he cannot deny Himself. He remained a lamb without blemish. Jesus is the Righteous One, and we are saved because of his righteousness.

There is no mention about how righteous the family members of Noah were, only of Noah's righteousness. The fact that the Lord repented that he even created man is evident of how evil had entered the hearts of all. There were eight individuals in the ark, and this family would go out from the ark and replenish the earth. God provided a way to save Noah and his family. The salvation of souls is important to God. When the Lord said that He would send a flood to destroy all flesh, he did not mention souls or their destiny. Since only Noah was righteous, it would appear that his family received mercy because of Noah's righteousness. Among the justified there is the Righteous One, and those who accept Divine Mercy. The remaining are left to face Divine Justice.

Chapter II

Fire and Brimstone

Lot's Home—Four Individuals Preserved Their Lineage

The second story of destruction and salvation is the story of Sodom and Gomorrah. Salvation came to Lot and his family, but the people of Sodom and Gomorrah perished when their cities were destroyed by fire and brimstone. Lot was Abram's nephew and had been with him most likely since the death of Lot's father, Haran. They left their native land, Ur of the Chaldeans, to go to the land of Canaan, but settled in Haran. Terah was the father of Abram and the grandfather of Lot. When Terah died, Abram continued to live in his father's house, until he was called by God.

The Lord called Abram to go forth from the land of his kinsfolk and from his father's house to another land, the land of Canaan. This is the covenant that the Lord made with Abram:

"I will make of you a great nation,
and I will bless you;
I will make your name great,
so that you will be a blessing.

> I will bless those who bless you
> and curse those who curse you.
> All the communities of the earth
> shall find blessing in you."
> (Genesis 12:2-3)

Abram, his wife Sarai and and his nephew Lot set out for the land of Canaan. They moved through the land of Canaan in stages, and when the Lord appeared to him, Abram would build an altar to the Lord. When famine struck the land of Canaan, Abram took his family to Egypt. By the time Abram left Egypt, he was very rich in livestock, silver and gold.

Lot, who went with Abram, also had flocks and herds and tents, so that the land could not support them if they stayed together; their possessions were so great that they could not dwell together. There were quarrels between the herdsmen of Abram's livestock and those of Lot's.

So Abram said to Lot: "Let there be no strife between you and me, or between your herdsmen and mine, for we are kinsmen. Is not the whole land at your disposal? Please separate from me. If you prefer the left, I will go to the right; if you prefer the right, I will go to the left." Lot looked about and saw how well watered the whole Jordan Plain was as far as Zoar, like the Lord's own garden, or like Egypt. Lot therefore chose for himself the whole Jordan Plain and set out eastward. (Genesis 13:5-12)

This is the reason they separated. *"Their possessions were so great that they could not live together."* Notice what Abram asked Lot: *"Is not the whole land at your disposal?"* Abram knew that the blessings came from the Lord. Although the blessings came through Abram, he offered Lot the opportunity to choose whatever he preferred. Of course, Lot chose what reminded him of the Lord's own garden or Egypt; paradise or the place of refuge during famine. Abram and his household prospered when the land was well watered. They prospered also while living in Egypt, but their prosperity was not due to well-watered land or the Egyptians, who gave Abram flocks and herds, male and female slaves, male and female asses and camels. They prospered because of the Lord and the covenant he made with Abram.

Sometimes when our possessions become so great, what was a blessing becomes a curse. I used the word "curse," to indicate being banished. We banish ourselves from the source of the blessings. This happens when the gift becomes more important than the giver.

When Abram was ninety-nine years old, the Lord appeared to him and said: "I am God the Almighty. Walk in my presence and be blameless. Between you and me I will establish my covenant, and I will multiply you exceedingly."

When Abram prostrated himself, God continued to speak to him. "My covenant with you is this: you are to become the father of a host of nations. No longer shall you be called Abram: your name shall be Abraham, for I am making you the father of a host of nations. I will render you exceedingly fertile; I will make nations of you; kings shall stem from you.

"This is my covenant with you and your descendants after you that you must keep: every male among you shall be circumcised."

God further said to Abraham: "As for your wife Sarai, do not call her Sarai; her name shall be Sarah. I will bless her, and I will give you a son by her. Him also will I bless; he shall give rise to nations, and rulers of peoples shall issue from him." (Genesis 17:1-6, 10, 15-16)

The Lord had blessed Abraham with so many possessions that the blessings overflowed to Lot. But here the Lord made it clear that there is another part of the covenant that is more valuable than all the material possessions. The greatest part of the blessings are the souls that would make up the Kingdom of God. This is an eternal kingdom, and the reward for Abraham's faithfulness is eternal.

When the Lord appeared to Abraham the next time, he appeared as three men. One of them revealed to Abraham and Sarah that he would return about the same time next year, and Sarah would have a son.

Then the Lord said: "The outcry against Sodom and Gomorrah is so great, and their sin so grave, that I must go down and see whether or not their actions fully correspond to the cry against them that comes to me. I mean to find out." (Genesis 18:20-21)

Immediately Abraham began to intercede for the people of Sodom. And the conversation ended with the Lord promising that if He found ten righteous people in the city, he would not destroy it. Two of the men went down to see if the evil in Sodom was as bad as was reported. Lot was sitting at the gate of Sodom.

When Lot saw them, he got up to greet them; and bowing down with his face to the ground, he said, "Please gentlemen, come aside into your servant's house for the night, and bathe your feet; you can get up early to continue your journey." (Genesis 19:1-2)

He persuaded them to stay at his home instead of the city square. During the night, the men of Sodom came and demanded that Lot's guests come out so that the men of Sodom could have intimacies with them. After threatening a forced entry, his guests pulled Lot into the house and closed the door;

at the same time, they struck the men at the entrance of the house, with such a blinding light that they were utterly unable to reach the doorway.

Here is a clear example of how the Lord blinds Satan, and that the Flame of Love is for the preservation of the family. Satan wants to destroy the family in our time as in all times past. Satan was blinded by the light in Lot's home, and that light is the Lord. The wicked perished in the flood waters, and the wicked perished in the fire and brimstone. Lot and his family escaped in time. They escaped because Lot had invited the Lord into his home. As one praying fervently, he pleaded and insisted that the Lord stay at his house.

Lot and his wife and two daughters left the cities and ran to safety. Scripture reveals that Lot's wife looked back and turned into a pillar of salt, while Lot and his daughters became the ancestors of the Moabite and the Ammonite peoples. Even though Sodom and Gomorrah were destroyed by fire and brimstone, Moab and Ammon represent how sin remains in the world until the end of time, but God does not abandon the human race. No matter how perverse and evil humanity becomes, God seems to always look for ways to save us.

Chapter III

The Red Sea

Moses and the Israelites Crossed the Red Sea

The third story of destruction and salvation is the story of the Israelites crossing the Red Sea. After Israel was set free from slavery in Egypt, Pharaoh changed his mind and pursued the Israelites. The Egyptians endured ten plagues in a battle against the Lord, God of the universe. The last plague was the death of the firstborn of Egypt, man and beast. Pharaoh admitted defeat, and he realized that neither he nor the gods of Egypt could not win a war against the Almighty God and Creator. Perhaps this story reveals that fallen angels cannot repent. Their hatred for God will perpetuate into eternity. Although Pharaoh is a human being, his story reflects how human behavior mirrors who we serve. Anyone who sets himself up as an enemy of God has joined the rebellion of the fallen angels. Even when Pharaoh accepted the fact that he had lost the war, he still preferred to see the Israelites destroyed. Sure, there were political and economic repercussions, but spiritually the fallen angels will not benefit from more people being damned along with themselves. There is nothing to gain but a larger kingdom of losers, but as the old adage goes, "misery loves company."

Rather than see the Israelites march away to serve the God of Abraham, Isaac and Jacob, Pharaoh preferred to slaughter them. Jesus said that the devil comes to scatter, slaughter and devour. Those who serve the devil and carry out his will desire the same things their master desires.

As the Israelites made their way through the Red Sea, the angel of the Lord guided their way to safety by giving them light. Simultaneously the angel blinded the Egyptian army by putting them in total darkness. God saved his people by blinding their enemies. The Israelites were in an invisible ark coming through the Red Sea. The waters came back together after the Israelites had made it safely to shore. The Egyptians drowned in the Red Sea because they were blinded and could not find their way out. The flood waters destroyed all flesh as in the flood of Noah's time. Water and fire, symbols of baptism in these three stories, represent two things: destruction and salvation. The waters and fire destroyed, but God saves. God saved Noah and his family, Lot and his family and Moses and his family, the Israelites.

Chapter IV

Mount Sinai

MOSES AND THE LEVITES REDEEMED THE FIRSTBORN

THE NEXT THREE STORIES ARE about fire and water. However, the fire and water do not represent destruction, but instead represent the awesome power of the One who saves.

Moses told the Israelites that God would appear to them in three days. He would appear on Mount Sinai, the same mountain that the burning bush appeared before Moses. The Lord had said to Moses: *"Come, now! I will send you to Pharaoh to Lead my people, the Israelites, out of Egypt."*

But Moses said to God, *"Who am I that I should go to Pharaoh and lead the Israelites out of Egypt?" He answered, "I will be with you; and this shall be your proof that it is I who have sent you: when you bring my people out of Egypt, you will worship God on this very mountain."* (Exodus 3:10-12.) The time had arrived for this promise to be fulfilled. Moses instructed the people to prepare themselves to meet God in three days. He said, Sanctify yourselves, wash your clothes and do not have intercourse with any woman. They were to prepare themselves to be a dwelling place for the Lord. God would dwell in their midst. They were to sanctify themselves and wash their clothes as a means of cleansing the temple. God would also change the way they worship.

When Adam and Eve were cast out of Paradise, it was to cleanse the temple. Since they were not willing to repent, they had to be expelled from the place of worship. God changed the way they worshiped by not permitting them to eat from the Tree of Life. Instructions about how to worship are not mentioned in Scripture, although something must have been sacrificed to cover their loins. The emphasis was on the way of sustaining their lives and preserving the human race through sexual reproduction. Adam and Eve went from having a means of worship, to having it stripped from them. In reality, they were the ones who rejected the Lord God and the way pointed out to them. The Lord cleansed the temple by casting them out of Paradise and changed the way that they worship by preventing them access to the Tree of Life.

The Lord was changing the way the Israelites worshiped, and this would set them apart from all other peoples of the world. All the descendants of Adam and Eve have their own ways of worship, but here on Mount Sinai, God gave to the Israelites a religious liturgy. God dictated to them exactly how they were to worship. So what was taken away from Adam and Eve is being restored to Moses and Israel.

Israel saw the mighty deeds done in Egypt to help them understand that there is only one God. When God revealed Himself as fire covering the entire mountain, He also revealed his identity by speaking to them. *"I, the Lord, am your God, who brought you out of the land of Egypt, that place of slavery. You* shall not have other gods besides me." (Exodus 20:2-3.) When Moses came to the people and related all the words and ordinances of the Lord, they all answered with one voice, "We will do everything that the Lord has told us." (Exodus 24:3.)

Israel was now accountable for her actions. God revealed Himself to them and they were instructed to worship God alone. Any other worship was considered false and to false gods. By the time Moses came down from the mountain with the plans for the tabernacle and instructions on how to offer sacrifice, the Israelites had made a golden calf and were worshiping it. The Lord told Moses to step aside so that He could wipe out these people, then He would begin a new people with Moses. Moses immediately began to intercede for the people as did Abraham for the people of Sodom. God listened to Moses and decided not to exterminate them.

Moses however, put them to a test. He ground the calf into dust, placed it in the water and made the people drink it. Then he said, *"Whoever is for the Lord, let him come to me!"* All the Levites rallied to him, and he told them, *"Thus says the Lord, the God of Israel: Put your sword on your hip, every one of you! Now go up and down the camp, from gate to gate, and slay your own kinsmen, your friends and neighbors!"* The Levites carried out the command of Moses, and that day there fell about three thousand of the people. (Exodus 32:26-28.) The test that Moses gave them appears to be "The Ordeal for a Suspected Adulteress" (Numbers 5:11-31.)

The Lord said that the Levites would redeem the firstborns. This is the first time we hear the word "redeem" in these episodes. The people were not put to death by the fire, as at Sodom and Gomorrah. The fire on the mountain was the presence of

God, and they were instructed not to touch the mountain and to keep a safe distance. If anyone touched the mountain, that person must be put to death by their fellow Israelites. The elements of water and fire destroyed lives and property in the flood, Sodom and Gomorrah and the Red Sea. It was not so with the fire on Mount Sinai.

Concerning the firstborn that were put to death by the Levites, their story seems to reflect the story of Cain and Abel, but with a different outcome. Cain murdered his brother Abel because God accepted Abel and his sacrifice, but God did not accept Cain or his sacrifice. This angered Cain, because Cain was the firstborn. After Cain killed Abel, God cast Cain out from His presence. *Cain said to the Lord, "My punishment is too great to bear. Since you have now banished me from the soil, and I must avoid your presence and become a restless wanderer on the earth, anyone may kill me at sight." "Not so!" The Lord said to him. "If anyone kills Cain, Cain shall be avenged sevenfold." So the Lord put a mark on Cain, lest anyone should kill him at sight.* (Genesis 4:13-15.)

I relate this to the firstborns who were guilty in pressing Aaron to make the calf. If Aaron was afraid they would kill him, as Cain did Abel, then the firstborns bear some responsibility for Aaron not entering the Promised Land. I am not sure if the Israelites understood the concept of being martyred at that time in history. Aaron would have done what it took to save his life. Why is this important? Because Aaron had been appointed high priest. The young bulls sacrificed were acceptable to God. Aaron's symbolic death was avenged by the avenger of blood, his family. There was a mark put on the three thousand firstborn that drank the water with the gold dust. They were cursed, and anyone could recognize the effect of the curse. The outcome was the opposite of Cain, who received a mark which prevented anyone from killing him, whereas these firstborn received a mark so that they could be put to death. Yet they were redeemed by the Levites. They were the ones who would lead the priestly people in the worship.

The next group that did not make it to the Promised Land became restless wanderers all the days of their lives. They wandered aimlessly in the desert for forty years, until all of them had died. This is another story that mirrors the punishment that Cain received, but their offense was quite the opposite of Cain's offense. This group was God's military; everyone that was twenty years of age or older at the time of the census. The reason they were destined to die in the desert is because they were unwilling to fight for the Lord and themselves.

The Lord said to Moses, "Send men to reconnoiter the land of Canaan, which I am giving the Israelites. You shall send one man from each ancestral tribe, all of them princes." So Moses dispatched them from the desert of Paran, as the Lord had ordered. (Numbers 13:1-3.) Upon their return, ten of the scouts gave a report that the people there were giants, who lived in fortified cities, and the Israelites were like grasshoppers to these giants. These men spread fear among the people and caused them to revolt. So they said among themselves, "Let us appoint a leader and go back to Egypt." The Lord threatened to wipe them out and begin a new people with Moses, but Moses interceded for them and God decided not to put them to death. Among the twelve scouts, only Joshua and Caleb were convinced that they should trust God and take possession of the land. Since these people were God's military, but were of no use to the kingdom, they were not allowed to enter the Promised Land. They were not willing to take possession of the land. Different from Cain in that they would not shed blood; they were more of the ideology of, "live and let die." The Lord allowed them to live, and let them die off in the desert over a period of forty years—a year for each day of the reconnaissance. They were restless wanderers, as was Cain. The firstborn of God's military was redeemed by those who were younger than twenty years at the time of the census. These were the ones who crossed over the Jordan into the Promised Land, destined to take possession of the land and become the kingdom of God.

Chapter V

The Jordan River

JOSHUA AND THE ISRAELITES CROSSED THE JORDAN RIVER

WHEN ISRAEL CAME TO THE Jordan River, they were given instructions about how they were to cross the river. *"When you see the ark of the covenant of the Lord, your God, which the Levitical priests will carry, you must also break camp and follow it, that you may know the way to take, for you have not gone over this road before. But let there be a space of two thousand cubits between you and the ark. Do not come nearer to it."* Joshua also said to the people, *"Sanctify yourselves, for tomorrow the Lord will perform wonders among you."* (Joshua 3:3-5.)

The people struck their tents to cross the Jordan, with the priests carrying the ark of the covenant ahead of them. No sooner had these priestly bearers of the ark waded into the waters at the edge of the Jordan, which overflows its banks during the entire season of the harvest, than the waters flowing from upstream halted backing up in a solid mass for a very great distance indeed, from Adam, a city in the direction of Zarethan; while those flowing downstream toward the Salt Sea of the Arabah disappeared entirely. (Joshua 3:15-16.)

The priests carrying the ark of the covenant of the Lord remained motionless on dry ground in the bed of the Jordan until the whole nation had completed the passage.

The contents inside of the ark of the covenant foreshadowed God incarnate in Jesus Christ. The Commandments written by God on the stone tablets, the jar of manna and the staff of Aaron the high priest all represent Jesus. The water had to part before the ark, because the ark represents the sacred space where God made his dwelling. God who is pure spirit became flesh and dwelled in His own creation. The mystery of the Incarnation is foreshadowed in the ark of the covenant. The elements of nature that had claimed the life of human beings are no threat to humans when they follow God into the elements, be it fire or water.

Once the Israelites had crossed over the Jordan, they were ready to begin to take possession of the land. It was time to drive out the wicked nations that lived in the land of Canaan and claim this land as the Kingdom of God. After crossing the Jordan, the Israelite nation was circumcised for the second time, because none of them born in the desert during the journey were circumcised. They celebrated the Passover on the evening of the fourteenth of the month. On that same day after the Passover on which they ate the produce of the land, the manna ceased.

Even Moses was not allowed to enter the Promised Land. He was allowed to look on the land from the top of Mount Nebo, but he did not enter with the Israelites that crossed the Jordan. Joshua succeeded Moses as judge and leader of the people.

Chapter V: The Jordan River | 33

That day when the Jordan River parted, the Lord began to exalt Joshua before the people, and they began to believe in Joshua as they had Moses.

Joshua had been a successful military commander; we may assume he was highly respected, but now he had become leader of the people of God. The first mission came soon, when they were instructed to destroy the city of Jericho. With direct and specific instructions from the Lord about how to take the city, the Israelites were successful.

Everything in salvation history was leading to God making His dwelling among His people. The tabernacle was called the Dwelling. The Holy of Holies in the temple was considered the dwelling place for God among His people. There was finally a permanent dwelling place for God where all peoples and nations could come to learn about the God of Abraham, Isaac and Jacob. Israel was meant to be a city on a hill, and a light to the nations. Their mission was to lead all peoples back to God, the Creator of the universe. There is one thing standing in the way of success: sin. A simple three-letter word is the cause of all failure to reunite the family of humanity with its Creator.

In Egypt, Israel watched God fight their battles for them. There was nothing for Israel to do but watch and be amazed at the awesome power and might of God, as He defeated the gods of Egypt. Things began to change when Israel had to join in the fight for their salvation. Everything had to be done precisely the way that God instructed them. First, their worship was dictated by God. Whom they worshiped, determined how and where they worshiped. Their first encounter with strict observance of a liturgical rite was the first Passover. Everything had to be done according to the instructions that God laid out. Their lives depended on it, and they were saved from death.

As Israel moved through the desert, we begin to see how rebellious humanity is, and it became clearer as to why they ended up as slaves in Egypt in the first place. It appears that God is using the story of Israel to reveal the story of all of humanity. Whatever God does to save us works perfect—but when we have to participate in the work of our salvation, things begin to fall apart, and even fail. The Israelites suffered through this during their forty-year journey to the land of Canaan. In their first expedition after crossing the Jordan, Israel was successful. They destroyed the city of Jericho as the Lord had instructed them to. Imagine if a military battle today had instructions to march around a city seven times, and after each time blow their trumpets! "After the seventh time everyone blow their trumpets, and the others shout!" In our world, the troops would wonder if their commander was trying to get them killed. But this worked for Israel; the wall of this fortified city collapsed and Israel accomplished what God sent them to accomplish.

It is evident that if the Israelites did what God commanded them, they would have been successful in all their battles and would have taken possession of the land. God is always faithful, but Israel was faithful sometimes. Other times they sinned and gave power to their enemies, especially when they began to worship the gods of their enemies. The whole period when the Israelites were ruled by judges reveals their success when they were obedient to God and failure when they were disobedient. God was their King and it was impossible for them to lose a battle if they followed the instructions of their King. When they obeyed the commands of the Lord, they lived in freedom. When they rebelled against the Lord, their enemies would come and take them captives. Israel suffered oppression many times at the hands of the Philistines. Each time when they repented their sins, and cried out to God for freedom, He sent a judge to defeat their enemies and set them free. Israel became tired of being judged by God for their sins and decided they wanted a king. All the other nations had kings and they wanted to be judged by a king also.

Samuel was displeased when they asked for a king to judge them. He prayed to the Lord, however, who said in answer: "Grant the people's every request. It is not you they reject, they are rejecting me as their king." (1 Samuel 8:6-7.)

The period of being judged by kings was plagued by the same disease: sin. And because of the sins of Solomon, the kingdom was split; north and south, with Israel in the north and Judah in the south. Israel worshiped the gods of their enemies and were finally destroyed as a nation in 722 B.C. by the Assyrians. Judah followed Israel's example and was destroyed as a nation by the Babylonians when taken into exile. Judah even disobeyed God by trying to fight against the Babylonians. The Lord had said, they must go and serve the king of Babylon and they would be allowed to return in seventy years. But the false prophets told them to rebel against the king of Babylon and promised them victory. As with all false prophesy, it was a lie and the Babylonians destroyed the temple. They were allowed to return to Jerusalem and rebuild the temple after seventy years, but Judah no longer existed as a nation. After the Babylonian exile, they were known only as the Jews.

From that time on the Jews were struggling to live peacefully among warring nations whose main objective was to rule the world. The known world was conquered by Alexander the Great.

The Greeks went as far as forcing the Jews to worship the Greek gods. The next great conquerors were the Romans, and this period leads us to the birth of our Savior Jesus Christ. The Jews and all of humanity needed a savior. God Himself came down from heaven to save His people as He did when He saved the Israelites from slavery in Egypt.

By the time of Jesus' birth, the Jews were awaiting their savior. This savior would be called Messiah. He would be someone like King David, even from the lineage of David. The Jews had been without a king for centuries and they were ready to be restored as a nation. King Herod took the same approach as the Pharaoh of Egypt by killing all the baby boys in Jerusalem. Herod knew that the newborn King of the Jews was the rightful claimant of the throne of David. This King would save his people from slavery to the Romans and all other so called rulers of the world.

There was one thing standing in the way of freedom: sin. Sin is the reason why all of humanity suffers bondage, and the Jews were no different. They were different in the sense that God revealed Himself to them. They were God's chosen people, but God expected them to avoid sin as much as everyone else, and even more so. To whom more is given, more is required. Whether it appears fair to humans or not, the Jews were held at a higher standard than the Gentiles. You may say the Gentiles were dependent upon the Jews for salvation. Jesus made this clear to the Samaritan woman at the well. He said, "You people worship what you do not understand; we worship what we understand, because salvation is from the Jews."

One thing is evidently clear: by the time Jesus began his public ministry, Israel had not taken full possession of the land of

Canaan. It was called the Promised Land because God promised that this land would become theirs. Yet, they would only possess the land if they obeyed the commands of the Lord.

When Jesus began his public ministry, one of the first things noticeable is that many people themselves had become possessed. Jesus began to free those who were possessed. Everyone Jesus freed from demonic possession seemed appreciative. Everyone Jesus healed from illnesses seemed appreciative. He gave sight to the blind, hearing to the deaf and healed the lame and those crippled. Everyone appeared happy and satisfied until Jesus said, "Your sins are forgiven." Now we have a problem; because they see him as judge. They haven't had a judge since Samuel, and the Lord made it clear to Samuel, "It is not you they have rejected, it is me they have rejected." The people of God decided that they did not want a judge. It was their way of rejecting God as judge over them. Well, it appears they were not ready to be judged. God Himself came down from heaven to save them as the judges did. This was acceptable in a military sense and also to heal their bodies, but to rule over their souls? Absolutely not.

Jesus would have to conquer their enemies alone, as the Lord did in Egypt when He defeated Pharaoh with the plagues. God did all of the work for the salvation of His people, while the people observed from the sideline. Jesus is responsible for the redemption of humanity. He did all the work up until He took his last breath on the cross. He freed Israel from slavery to the Law, but now they must begin the journey to take possession of the Promised Land. I am speaking of the New Israel, the Church.

After the death, burial and resurrection of our Lord Jesus Christ, the disciples were led to assume responsibility for the salvation of souls. This can only be accomplished if God is dwelling in their midst. Everything depends on this reality which Jesus began on the evening of the Resurrection and fulfilled on the day of Pentecost.

Chapter VI

The Upper Room

Peter and the Israelites Sent from the Upper Room

God began to make His dwelling with humanity; but in a different way than in the past. He dwelled in the meeting tent, called the tabernacle. After the temple was built, God dwelt in the Holy of Holies, but now God had made His dwelling again in movable tabernacles. At Pentecost, God began to dwell in the soul of His disciples, making each disciple a movable tabernacle.

Let's recount this glorious and most important event. The disciples were all in one place praying and waiting for the Holy Spirit, as per the instruction of Jesus, when suddenly they heard the sound of rushing wind, and tongues of fire descended from above, beginning to split and rest on the head of each of them, until they were all filled with the Holy Spirit. The disciples, who were all Galileans, began speaking to the crowd and everyone heard them speaking in his own language, no matter what language they spoke. Pentecost—the defeat of Babel and the confusion of languages—is the beginning of uniting all nations under one God. There is only one language in the Church, because there is only one Spirit of Truth, the Holy Spirit. And as Jesus said, "Everyone who belongs to the truth, hears his voice." The twelve disciples were sent from the upper room as apostles. This is the moment they were waiting for. Jesus told them to wait until they received power from on high; the Holy Spirit whom He would send in a few days.

The Church received the promised Holy Spirit, and from that moment on they began to set the earth on fire. This is the moment that Jesus longed for; the birth of the Church. Tongues of fire meant that the teaching and preaching would set the earth on fire. As the Church took possession of the land on the seven continents, the lies of false gods were burned up by the consuming fire of God. Most of the world heard the Good News preached to them. Mass conversions took place and replaced the pagan worship which had been established by the fallen angels. There is only one thing that could impede the New Israel from taking possession of the whole earth. If you guessed sin, you are correct. There would never be a complete fallout as the descendants of Adam and Eve, or even being destroyed as Israel and Judah were. We know this because of Jesus' promise to Peter. He said that the gates of hell shall not prevail against His Church. This means that the Holy Spirit would not leave them orphans, and they would always be able set the earth on fire with their teaching and preaching. But sin prevents listeners from hearing Jesus voice as was heard on the day of Pentecost. This causes divisions and even major schisms, regardless of who is credited with the blame.

Jesus is still responsible for the redemption of humanity, because He is the Redeemer. However, beginning with the day of Pentecost, Jesus commands us to participate in His work of redemption. Every disciple goes out to evangelize as an individual with Almighty God dwelling within his soul. This is how we begin to participate in the work of redemption, just as the Israelites began to participate after they left Egypt. All of the work in Egypt was accomplished by God alone, and all of the work of Jesus' Passion was accomplished by Jesus alone. Now it was time for Israel to take possession of the land, and it could only be accomplished by obedience to God. Obedience first in worship as defined by God, and secondly in every word that proceeds from the mouth of God. Whoever does not recognize what is meant by the mouth of God, cannot hear His voice. Just as John the Baptist was the voice of one crying in the wilderness, "Repent and be baptized for the forgiveness of your sins." John is the last of a cycle of prophets that began with Elijah.

There is a New Testament cycle of prophets that began with St. Peter. It began with St. Peter saying, "Repent and be baptized in the name of Jesus Christ for the forgiveness of your sins, and you will receive the gift of the Holy Spirit." This is the voice of one crying in the wilderness to prepare the way of the second coming of Christ. When John the Baptist began crying out in the wilderness, Jesus was already dwelling in their midst. When St. Peter began crying out on the day of Pentecost, Jesus was already dwelling in their midst, this time in spirit.

Sometimes even disciples become deaf, and even refuse to see. They will no longer hear Jesus' voice, because they no longer belong to the truth. But Jesus has an answer for a dilemma as such. His answer is a new Pentecost: the Flame of Love of the Immaculate Heart of Mary.

PART II—FROM PENTECOST TO BEGINNING

Chapter VII

House of the Carmelite Fathers

I INVITE THOSE LIVING IN THE HOUSE OF THE CARMELITE FATHERS—THE UPPER ROOM

Let them be the first to receive the Flame of Love to spread it.

THE NEW PENTECOST ADDED A miraculous wonder to the work of the tongues of fire. It added the Flame of Love of the Immaculate Heart of Mary. Those living in the house of the Carmelite fathers were the first to receive the Flame of Love and to spread it. It is that place where God allows the breath of life to return to us. In the case of Elijah, it was both the upper room and the upper chamber of the soul. Elijah stayed in the upper room when he lived with the widow of Zarephath and her son. He is the first of the Carmelite fathers, and also the first of a cycle of prophets that ended with John the Baptist.

When the son of the widow died, Elijah took his body to the upper room, and prayed that God would allow the life breath to return to the child. God answered his prayer, and the soul of the boy returned to his body. Elijah took the child downstairs and gave him to his mother, and said to her, "See! Your son is alive."

The widow believed her sin to be the cause of her son's death. After her son was raised back to life, she believed Elijah to be a man of God, and that the word of the Lord came truly from His mouth—it became obvious that God is truth, and He is the Lord and giver of life. We may conclude also that the devil is the father of lies and the author of death. But the story itself foreshadows Elijah uniting all of Israel on Mount Carmel, and bringing them back to their senses. The Israelites came to the realization that the false prophets were keeping them in bondage to the father of lies. To reunite with God, who is truth, is to be raised from the dead.

That is the story of Elijah and Mount Carmel, but the story does not end there. Nor does it end with the last prophet of the Old Testament, John the Baptist. Elijah was united with the Blessed Virgin Mary when she visited Elizabeth. In the mystery of the Visitation, the Blessed Virgin Mary assumed her role over the office of prophecy. Her role in the story of Mount Carmel is evident, as revealed first with the Brown Scapular and now with the Flame of Love. She gave the Brown Scapular to us in this way: *Our Lady of Mount Carmel appeared to Carmelite Monk Saint Simon Stock in 1251 and presented him with a brown wool scapular, saying, "Whoever dies invested with this Scapular shall be preserved from the eternal flames. It is a sign of salvation, a sure safeguard in danger, a pledge of peace and of my special protection until the end of the ages."*

John the Baptist received the gift of new life from within his mother's womb. Elizabeth and the child in her womb were filled with the Holy Spirit at the sound of Mary's greeting. It is God who gives life; Jesus raised the infant to life by the forgiveness of sin. Here the upper room is the womb, and Mary is the voice. Jesus however, is the Alpha and the Omega, the first and the last, the beginning and the end.

The last group of Carmelite fathers from the Old Testament were disciples of John the Baptist. These men later became disciples of Jesus. On the evening of the Resurrection, Jesus entered the upper room although the doors were locked. He breathed on the disciples and said, "Peace be with you. Receive the Holy Spirit." These fathers were the first to receive the Holy Spirit from the Resurrected Christ, and they were the first to confer the Holy Spirit through the Sacraments, and by the imposition of hands.

The Carmelite fathers in Hungary are the twelve priests that Jesus chose. They would be the first to receive and spread the Flame of Love. Twelve priests and their twelve churches respectively are like the twelve apostles and the disciples in the upper room at the first Pentecost; about one hundred and twenty disciples total. Twelve priests and twelve churches simultaneously began to spread the Flame of Love in Hungary. Jesus chose the feast of Candlemas as the feast day of the Flame of Love. The first solemn procession in Hungary would be the sign that the Flame of Love was going out from twelve churches simultaneously. The candles remind us of the tongues of fire on the heads of the disciples on the first Pentecost.

We must remember that the Most Holy Trinity gave the effusion of the Flame of Love to the Blessed Virgin Mary, and she gave the Flame of Love to Elizabeth Kindelmann. From Elizabeth Kindelmann one priest would receive the gift and take the cause to the twelve priests. If all of this sounds familiar, it is because it reflects the story of the Incarnation, the Visitation, and John baptizing the twelve apostles. The story of the first Pentecost has been made present in our time, with the gift of the Flame of Love.

The Flame of Love must spread first in Hungary, like the first Pentecost, in which Jesus had instructed his disciples to go out first to Jerusalem. From there they were commissioned to go to Judea, Samaria and the surrounding areas, then to the ends of the earth. They were to spread the Flame of Love in Hungary first, because Hungary was the Promised Land. However, this time the Israelites journeyed across the Jordan back into the wilderness. What I am saying is that the journey to spread the Flame of Love to the world is the same route that the children of Israel took to get to the Promised Land.

Once the New Israel had taken possession of the Promised Land, they crossed the Jordan and went back into the wilderness, and from there journeyed back to Egypt.

This movement of the Flame of Love is in reverse order, going back to the beginning. However, no matter how perplexing it may be, it must be viewed looking forward and backward. For example, going forward it is about the Holy Spirit. Elijah is not portrayed as having the indwelling of the Holy Spirit. Scripture says that the Holy Spirit came upon him. So when Elijah stretched over the widow's son three times and the soul of the child returned to his body, we may look at this as the work of the Holy Spirit which was upon Elijah, including Elijah's cloak as a symbol of the Brown Scapular.

The infant John the Baptist in his mother's womb, however, was filled with the Holy Spirit. For the first time we see Jesus through Mary give Himself to others. Elizabeth and the child in her womb were filled with the Holy Spirit.

On the evening of the Resurrection when Jesus came into the upper room and breathed on the disciples, they received the indwelling of the Holy Spirit as did Elizabeth and her child.

The house of the Carmelite fathers has multiple meanings. One of great importance is the interior life. The interior life is, as it was for the first man when the Lord God blew into his nostrils the breath of life, and the man became a living being.

Once man sinned, the breath would return to God and the man would return to the earth. The house of the Carmelite fathers is about restoring the interior life of the spirit that was lost because of sin. Notice the widow asked Elijah, "Have you come to me to call attention to my guilt and to kill my son?" Meaning her sin was the cause of death to her son. I touched on this in the book, *Unity and the Flame of Love*. I related this story to St. John of the Cross and the Dark Night, but did not go into detail. Perhaps it is time to go a little deeper into this mystery.

The widow can be referred to as the woman who ate the forbidden fruit. She gave the fruit to her husband and he ate of it also. This caused his spiritual death, and spiritually she became widowed. Why do I say she became widowed? Because their marriage was one of a prophet and prophetess. Life came from God to the man, and through the man to the woman. The breath of life to his nostrils brings life to his body. The Word of God to his ears remains in the head to govern the body. But sin and death came from the serpent to the woman, and through her to the man. He died a spiritual death as the prophet, so the woman is a prophetess without a husband. Since she gave him what she thought was the way to eternal life, spiritually she became his mother. And the man was reborn of the father of lies and the woman.

The Dark Night brings about the death of the woman in the drought of Elijah's time. She accepted that she would live by trusting what God revealed to her through the prophet Elijah. The Word of God is more important than what feeds the body, so she gave her last morsel of bread to the prophet. She was going through the Dark Night and it was revealed that her sin caused the death of her son.

Beginning the Dark Night of the Spirit, the prophets must suffer until attention is drawn to the sin of the first man, Adam. It was revealed in the story of Zechariah in the temple when he lost his voice. This is the story of Adam, who lost his voice as the prophet. Jesus came to Zechariah's house and filled Elizabeth and the child in her womb with the Holy Spirit. The child was set free of the original sin inherited at conception. Both the sensual and the spiritual, upper and lower chamber of the soul were brought into union with Jesus.

Concerning Zechariah and Elizabeth, Scripture says: *"Both were righteous in the eyes of God, observing all the commandments and ordinances of the Lord blamelessly."* (Luke 1:6.) All that was left for them was to be brought into the mystical marriage with Jesus, which appears to have occurred in the Joyful Mystery of the Visitation.

The house of the Carmelite fathers is where the Holy Spirit restored the breath of life to the widow's son after Elijah stretched over him three times. It is the house where the Holy Spirit filled the infant John the Baptist for three months before he was born. And the house of the Carmelite fathers is where the disciples were hiding for three days before Jesus breathed on them and said, "Receive the Holy Spirit." Prophetess, prophet and priests were restored. The apostles being priest were forgiven of actual sins whereas the prophet in the womb was forgiven the original sin that he inherited from his father, Adam. When Jesus said to the apostles, "Whose sins you forgive are forgiven them," He gave them the authority to function as priests. When He gave them the authority to retain sins, it is moreso the authority to guard the kingdom. Jesus is the King of kings and He did not die a spiritual death. Beginning on Palm Sunday before His Passion, Israel had accepted Jesus as their King. They had accepted God as their King once again. Although the prophetess, prophet and priests all died because of sin, God who is their king could not die a spiritual death; He gave up his body to be tortured and killed for the sins of the people.

When I speak of the New Israel traveling back to the beginning, they are journeying with all of the gifts they received going forward. Although they are headed back to the wilderness, they do so as a people baptized with water, the Holy Spirit and with fire. The only way that they or should I say *we* can take possession of the land, is if Jesus dwells within us. Jesus ask us to pray this way: "May our feet journey together, may our hands gather in unity."

This chart shows the pilgrimage that began with those who lived in the house of the Carmelite fathers. They were the first to receive the Flame of Love and spread it. The arrow points to the direction of the pilgrimage back to the beginning.

THE HOLY SPIRIT		
House of the widow of Zarephath	House of Elizabeth, wife of Zechariah	**House of Salome**
Elijah in the upper room *The soul returned to the boy*	Infant in the womb *Child filled with the Holy Spirit*	**Disciples in the upper room** ***Disciples received the Holy Spirit***

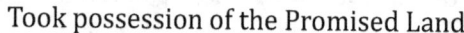

Took possession of the Promised Land

Chapter VIII

A New Instrument

I WOULD LIKE TO PLACE IN YOUR HANDS A NEW INSTRUMENT—CROSSING THE JORDAN

HUNGARY IS THE PROMISED LAND where the new evangelization began. The Blessed Virgin referred to Hungary as her country, and of her promise to Saint Stephen. The Most Holy Virgin said, "*King Saint Steven consecrated your country to me and I promised him that I would gather his intercession and that of the other Hungarian saints into my heart.*

"*I would like to place in your hands a new instrument, which I want you to accept and appreciate the importance of, because my heart looks upon my country with great affliction. The twelve priests whom my Divine Son chose will be the most worthy to fulfill my petition. Take this Flame, my daughter, you are the first one I am handing it to. Ignite your own heart with it and then pass it on to others.*" (Spiritual Diary of Elizabeth Kindelmann, page 27.)

Three incidents that reveal how God allows us to participate in our own redemption and the redemption of others are when the Israelites cross over areas of water. Going forward to the land of Canaan, the Israelites had to first escape death at the hands of Pharaoh and his army. The Lord had set Israel free from slavery in Egypt by overpowering the Egyptians with ten plagues. The first three were miracles that proved that the God of Israel is the true God, and there is no other god but He. The other seven miracles are actually plagues that overpowered the Egyptians. Once the war was over between God and the gods of Egypt, the Lord said, "I came to pass judgment on the gods of Egypt." God did all of the work to save Israel, and all Israel had to do was stand by and watch. As I mentioned earlier, the night of the first Passover brought the Israelites into active participation in the work of their salvation. Once God established that He is the true God and creator, He established how he is to be worshiped. The Passover requires their participation in the salvation of the firstborns, and they must continue to celebrate this liturgical feast as part of the covenant. Our participation in the Sacrifice of the Mass is also a memorial of death passing over the firstborns. The Divine Liturgy in the Christian tradition *"is the participation of the People of God in the work of God."* (Catechism of the Catholic Church—1069.)

From this point on Israel must actively participate, just as much as Christians must actively participate after the Pentecostal experience. When the Israelites were faced with the Red Sea and Pharaoh's military approaching them from the rear, Moses called out to the Lord to save them. But the Lord's response was, *"Why are you crying out to Me? You have the staff in your hand, hold it out in the direction of the sea and the waters will part."* The first part of the statement to Moses is startling. *"Why are you crying out to Me?"* (Exodus 14:15.) The staff was a new instrument that God had placed in the hands of Moses the prophet. The Flame of Love was a new instrument in the hands of Elizabeth Kindelmann. Jesus told her, *"Do not ask Me what to do. Be creative!"* (Spiritual Diary of Elizabeth Kindelmann, page 21.)

The next time the Israelites had to cross a channel of water was when they crossed the Jordan River. The instructions this time to Joshua was that the priests carrying the ark of the covenant should go ahead of the people. When the feet of the priests touched the water, the river parted as the Red Sea did for Moses. The four priests bore the ark on their shoulders, but they held the poles in their hands. God had placed a new instrument in their hands. In this way, the Lord required the priests to actively participate in the work of salvation. They crossed over into the land of Canaan to take possession of the land by driving out the evil nations that lived there.

In the Gospel of John, the story of the wedding feast at Cana reveals where all of this is headed. It all points to Jesus. This story shows how the people must participate by following Jesus' instructions, but it also shows that the Blessed Virgin Mary goes before us to intercede on our behalf. She is the ark in which Jesus dwelled first.

Jesus, his mother and four of his disciples were present at this celebration. We notice that the four disciples are different than the first four mentioned in the synoptic gospels. One of the reasons for this may be that the Gospel of John begins as the creation story and walks through salvation history quickly. Also, it appears to only walk us through those parts of the history that reveals our redemption, and not the fall or any of the stories that reveal the failures and sins that causes division. It seems to reveal mainly what Jesus is doing to redeem us in the context of a new creation. The four priests represent types of Christ in the Old Testament: Abel, Enosh, Isaac and Israel, symbolizing four priests carrying the ark. The ark goes before the people to help guarantee success or victory. Success or failure for the Israelites depends on whether they are obedient to God or not.

At the wedding feast at Cana, the Blessed Virgin Mary went before the people and interceded for them. She said to Jesus, "They have no wine." Then she interceded to the people to make clear the will of God. She said, *"Do whatever He tells you."* The attendants followed Jesus' instructions, which were to fill the jars with water, and then to draw some out and take it to the head waiter. When the head waiter tasted the wine which had been brought to him by the attendants, he came to the bridegroom and said, *"Everyone serves the good wine first, and then when people have drunk freely, an inferior one; but you have kept the good wine until now."* (John 2:10.)

As Jesus said in, The Book of Revelation: *"I am the Alpha and the Omega, the first and the last, the beginning and the end."* (Revelation 22:13.) The water jars for ritual washing refer moreso to the Law. Moses is the Law giver. Pharaoh's daughter said she named him Moses because she drew him out of the water. Jesus changed the water to wine and had the attendant to draw some out and take it to the head waiter to taste it. The waiter recognized that the new wine is superior; the New Testament fulfills the Old Testament. The Holy Spirit is freedom, but as St. Paul said, "the Law is slavery." The Flame of Love of the Immaculate Heart of Mary is freedom. It is an instrument used to free souls from slavery to the devil. *"Those accepting the Flame of Love will be intoxicated by the abundance of graces and they will proclaim everywhere, as I said before, that such a torrent of grace has never been granted since the Word became Flesh."* (Spiritual Diary of Elizabeth Kindelmann, page 175.) Jesus is the Word made flesh, and the Flame of Love.

Concerning the Flame of Love of the Immaculate Heart of Mary: the wedding feast at Cana portrays the Blessed Virgin Mary as the one who goes before the people and intercedes on our behalf. This story is the best example of how private revelation works. We are not obligated to believe private revelation and thus we are not obligated to obey instructions or even commands from private revelation. What we see at the wedding at Cana is not private revelation, but the sequential order in which things occurred falls in line with the Flame of Love diary. First the Blessed Virgin Mary pleaded on our behalf as she did for the wedding guest. Jesus said, *"It is exclusively thanks to the efficacious pleas of the Most Holy Virgin that the Most Holy Trinity granted the effusion of the Flame of Love."* (Spiritual Diary of Elizabeth Kindelmann, page 101.) She pleads with us to obey God, repent and avoid sin. This is similar to when she said, *"Do whatever he tells you."* Then Jesus tells us what to do if we want something done about being without wine for the celebration. To make the new wine was a gift from God and the people were not obligated to do anything to receive this gift. But with all private revelation there are request made to us with a promise of what we will receive if we fulfill the request. It is all done in good faith and trust in God and His saints. After receiving the gift of the Flame of Love, we can benefit from doing what Jesus and Mary request and receive what they promise, just as the attendants at the wedding filled the jars and received the new wine. They were not obligated to fill the jars, but because they trusted Jesus they received this wonderful gift of new wine.

The jars were empty, but then filled to the brim, just like the Jordan River which parted and after the people had crossed the waters overflowed the banks. Jesus' disciples began to believe in Him because God began to exalt Him as He did for Joshua after crossing the Jordan. Jesus allowed the people to participate in His work of redemption by placing a new instrument in their hands. They filled the jars with water.

The Blessed Virgin gave Elizabeth Kindelmann a new instrument in her hand. It is the Flame of Love from her Immaculate Heart. It goes from heart to heart, meaning in the soul, but it is also an instrument to blind Satan, so it is also referred to as an instrument to work with. Any work done refers to hands. Jesus gave Elizabeth an instrument to blind Satan, which we call the Unity Prayer.

May our feet journey together,
May our hands gather in unity,
May our hearts beat in unison,
May our souls be in harmony,
May our thoughts be as one,
May our ears listen to the silence together,
May our glances profoundly penetrate each other,
May our lips pray together to gain mercy from the Eternal Father.

The Blessed Virgin gave Elizabeth Kindelmann a prayer petition also, which she referred to as an instrument in her hand, which will blind Satan.

Hail Mary, full of grace, the Lord is with thee.
Blessed are thou among women, and blessed is the fruit of thy womb Jesus.

Holy Mary, Mother of God, pray for us sinners. Spread the effect of grace of thy Flame of Love, over all of humanity, Now and at the hour of our death. Amen

These gifts are given to us as instruments in our hands, used to blind Satan and free souls from his grips. The Flame of Love is in the soul, and the prayers are said with the lips or in our thoughts, but they are still considered instruments in our hands, because we are united as one with Jesus in the unity prayer. Body and soul become one with Jesus.

The Danube River is the point of reference that the Flame of Love has saved the country of Hungary. We see the government supporting marriage and encouraging citizens to procreate. This calls for trust in God. The government is offering financial incentives so that people will not be deterred from having a family, because of economic reasons. This is a great accomplishment, considering the damages that were done to this society by Nazism and Communism, both references to polytheism and atheism. Hungary has been saved, and I believe much of it should be credited to the Flame of Love of the Immaculate Heart of Mary.

The four churches in the capital city dedicated to the Blessed Virgin are the ark. The four priests who are pastors of these churches are the priests carrying the ark. Although Buda and Pest were united as one city by a bridge built in 1873, the true bridge is the ark carried by the four priests. The Danube River runs north and south and turns to run east and west into the sea. So crossing the Danube takes the Flame of Love in all directions to go out into the rest of the world. Cardinal Peter Erdo approved the Flame of Love movement for his diocese and gave an imprimatur to the Diary of Elizabeth Kindelmann. He later approved the statutes for the Flame of Love movement.

Speaking of water and fire, the cities of Buda and Pest appear to have special meaning in the names. One interpretation of the name Buda is water. Pest means furnace to refer to the burning caves where fire was kept alive. Very intriguing, considering the mystique of the Flame of Love.

The chart below shows how God placed an instrument in the hands of his servants. Now let's cross the Jordan and return to the wilderness.

Water		
The Red Sea	**The Jordan River**	**The six jars**
Moses parted the Red Sea *The Israelites crossed safely to the other side*	**The Jordan parted before the ark of the covenant** *The Israelites entered the Promised Land*	The Blessed Virgin interceded for the people *The guests were blessed to drink the new wine*

⬅

Chapter IX

From Mount Carmel

THE FLAME OF LOVE MUST GO FORTH FROM THE CARMEL—MOUNT SINAI

THE FLAME OF LOVE MOVEMENT made its way into the wilderness, also called the desert. The movement has to journey toward the ocean, which represents the Red Sea. There is symbolism here just as Mount Carmel and Mount Sinai are linked together in the story of Elijah. Yet, today we are not sure of what mountain was referred to as Mount Sinai for Moses and the Israelites. Here, I will relate Mount Carmel as the place where the Israelites were gathered to meet God, and acknowledge God as the only true God. This happened on Mount Sinai, Mount Carmel and in the upper room.

God appeared to the Israelites on Mount Sinai, in the desert. He appeared as a consuming fire that covered the mountain. The slavery in Egypt did not allow the Israelites to worship God as the only true God, because that would be an acclamation that the gods of Egypt were false gods. To reject the gods of Egypt would be to reject the Egyptian government, because there was no true separation between the pagan worship and their government.

The real issue for the Israelites was their rejection of the prophet Joseph. The patriarchs sold their brother Joseph into slavery because they were jealous of him. They intended to kill him as Cain did Abel, but Reuben talked them out of shedding blood. For this reason, they were held in bondage in Egypt, by people who created their own gods. By reason of default, to reject the prophet is to accept idolatry. When the Lord came down to meet them on Mount Sinai, it was to reveal Himself to them and give them the chance to accept the true God of the universe. And they did accept Him, for a short time.

This event revealed God on the mountain as in a consuming fire. There was the loud trumpet and God speaking with Moses. When God spoke, it sounded like thunder to the Israelites, but when Moses answered they understood him in their language. This ties into the Pentecostal experience when God spoke through men and everyone understood in their language, but no one understood the unknown tongue, except the one who uttered the message and the messenger. Regardless, the Israelites in the desert were impressed with what they heard and ratified the covenant saying, *"We will do everything that the Lord has told us."* (Exodus 24:3.) They also asked Moses to speak to them from then on, fearing that they could die from hearing God speak to them. The focal point is that they acknowledged that the Lord is God.

God came down to His people again, this time as a consuming fire on Mount Carmel. *Seeing this, all the people fell prostrate and said, "The Lord is God, the Lord is God."* (1 Kings 18:39.)

Elijah had told Ahab to gather all of Israel on Mount Carmel. He challenged the prophets of Baal to prove who is Lord of Israel. First he asked the people, "How long are you going to straddle the issue? Are you going to worship the Lord God of Israel or Baal?" And the people did not answer, but just looked at him. Then he challenged the prophets of Baal to offer a bull as sacrifice and he would offer one as well. And whoever sent down fire from heaven was the true God. The people said, "Agreed." Of course, nothing happened when Jezebel's prophets offered their bull. Elijah repaired the altar of twelve stones that had been torn down. Elijah had the bull he was to offer as sacrifice cut in pieces and poured twelve jars of water on it. *At the time for offering sacrifice, the prophet Elijah came forward and said, "Lord, God of Abraham, Isaac and Israel, let it be known this day that you are God in Israel and that I am your servant and have done all these things by your command. Answer me, Lord! Answer me, that this people may know that you, Lord, are God and that you have brought them back to their senses." The Lord's fire came down and consumed the holocaust, wood, stones and dust, and it lapped up the water in the trench. Seeing this, all the people fell prostrate and said, "The Lord is God, the Lord is God."* (I Kings 18:36-39.) The Israelites on Mount Carmel were convinced after seeing the sign, whereas the Israelites at Mount Sinai were convinced after hearing God speak. Both times the people were brought out of worshiping false gods and united with the God of Abraham, Isaac and Jacob.

The third time that Israel was brought together in this way was in the upper room on Pentecost Day. Twelve apostles and a total of about one hundred and twenty disciples were gathered in the upper room. *When the time for Pentecost was fulfilled, they* were all in one place together. And suddenly there came from the sky a noise like a strong driving wind, and it filled the entire house in which they were. Then there appeared to them tongues as of fire, which parted and came to rest on each of them. And they were all filled with the Holy Spirit and began to speak in different tongues, as the Spirit enabled them to proclaim. (Acts 2:1-4.)

The chart below may help visualize the three times that God appeared as fire and the people acknowledged Him as God.

FIRE		
Mount Sinai	Mount Carmel	The upper room
All of Israel heard God speak	All of Israel saw the sign	The Jews gathered for the feast understood the disciples in their language
The people ratified the covenant with God	The people acknowledged that the Lord is God	The people recognized Jesus as Savior

The Mount Carmel experience points to Mount Sinai in the desert.

These charts show how the Pentecostal experience became a reality in our time.

CHART 1—From the Carmel

FIRE		
Mount Sinai	Mount Carmel	The upper room
All of Israel heard God speak and believed The people ratified the covenant with God	All of Israel saw the sign and believed The people acknowledged that the Lord is God	Thomas said that he would not believe unless he touched Jesus' wounds with his hands Thomas said, "My Lord and my God"

CHART 2—Pentecostal Experience

FIRE		
The upper room	The temple	Cornelius' house
Jews from every nation under heaven heard God speak through the disciples About 3000 persons accepted baptism and were added that day	Jews in the temple saw the sign—the man at the beautiful gate healed The number of men in the church increased to about 5000	The Gentiles believed without seeing They received the gift of the Holy Spirit and God manifested signs

CHART 3—The New Pentecostal Experience

FIRE		
Bethel Bible—Topeka, Kansas	Duquesne—Pennsylvania	12 Churches—Hungary
Methodist minister and students prayed for baptism in the Spirit and tongues as evidence One student, Agnes Osman, began to speak in tongues—the movement began	Catholics went out to see the signs among the Protestants They asked to be initiated into the movement and began to speak in tongues	Catholics believed without seeing They received the gift of the Flame of Love and it is authenticated in the soul

Chart 1—From the Carmel

We have three charts to help visualize the great work of salvation that is taking place in our time. I used the Pentecostal experiences of Israel on Mount Sinai, on Mount Carmel and the upper room to show that the Israelites were pilgrims in a foreign land, and so are we. In the first chart, each time God revealed himself, the Israelites acknowledged that He is God and there is no other. However, when the disciples told Thomas that the Lord had appeared to them, Thomas replied, *"Unless I see the mark of the nails in his hands and put my finger into the nail-marks and put my hand into his side, I will not believe."* A week later, Jesus returned and allowed Thomas to physically touch his wounds. After touching Jesus' wounds, Thomas said, *"My Lord and my God!"* Jesus said to him, *"Have you come to believe because you have seen me? Blessed are those who have not seen and have believed."* (John 20:25, 28-29.)

Chart 2—Pentecostal Experience

The second chart shows the actual evangelization effects of Pentecost. On Pentecost Day, there were Jews and converts to Judaism from every nation under heaven. When the disciples began speaking, everyone understood them in their own language. They were Hellenists Jews, living in the Greek diaspora. They heard the wisdom of God. These people may have had synagogues in their areas, but they were separated from the temple where the sacrifices were offered.

Next, Peter and John went to the temple for the afternoon prayer and healed the man at the beautiful gate. The Jews in the temple saw the sign. The language in the temple is Hebrew. St. Paul later said that Greeks seek wisdom and Jews look for signs.

Later, when St. Peter went to the house of Cornelius the centurion and spoke to them about the Lord, while Peter was still speaking, the Holy Spirit fell upon all who were listening to the word. The circumcised believers could hear them speaking in tongues and glorifying God. These people believed by faith, without having to see. The church had become one: Hebrew, Latin and Greek. Each group accepted baptism after hearing St. Peter speak. This is how the Flame of Love is spread, by speech. We must tell people about it the way that St. Peter spoke to them about Jesus being the Savior. The Flame of Love is Jesus Christ himself.

CHART 3—THE NEW PENTECOSTAL EXPERIENCE

Our modern day experiences reveal a new Pentecost. On January 1, 1901, Methodist Minister Charles Parham and his students at Bethel Bible Study in Topeka, Kansas were praying for the baptism of the Holy Spirit to be experienced in their group. They had agreed that the sign would be speaking in tongues. When Minister Parham laid hands on Agnes Osman and prayed for her, she began speaking in tongues. Interestingly Pope Leo XIII and the bishops of the world had just finished a novena asking for a new Pentecost.

In 1967 some Catholic students at Duquesne University went to an Episcopalian prayer service to see the signs they had been hearing about. After seeing for themselves, they asked the prayer group to pray for them to receive this baptism, and this was the beginning of the Catholic Charismatic movement. Pope

St. John XXIII called Vatican II for a new Pentecost and evangelization. The counsel ended in 1965.

Pope St. Paul VI approved a Prayer of Propagation for the Flame of Love published in 1973, and the Flame of Love is spreading throughout the world. It will reach even the unbaptized, meaning this group must be like Cornelius and the uncircumcised. Blessed are those who have not seen and have believed. This miracle will not have to be authenticated by those in authority. It will be authenticated in the soul of each individual. In spite of this, the Flame of Love is still spread by speech.

It was the prayers of the popes that preceded each movement of this new Pentecost, just as it did when St. Peter spoke to each group during the first Pentecostal experiences. Although the popes ushered in the new Pentecost, everyone is responsible for spreading the Flame of Love of the Immaculate Heart of Mary. It is spread by speech and we have no right to be silent.

Since the Flame of Love must go forth from the Carmel and advance to Mount Sinai in the desert, the militant church will need help. *Jesus said: "The Church and the whole world is in grave danger. Even with your strength, you cannot change this situation. The Most Holy Trinity alone can help you, through the concerted intercession of the Most Blessed Virgin, all the angels, all the saints, and those souls whom you have freed from Purgatory."* (Spiritual Diary of Elizabeth Kindelmann, page 291.) The church militant is dependent on the help of the church triumphant and those we help to set free from the church suffering. The warriors who spent forty years in the desert until every one of them died off, died in the desert because they were not willing to fight. If any of these souls are in purgatory and we help to free them by observing the

Monday fast of bread and water, then they will join God's military again—this time as prayer warriors. There may be a logical reason why Pharaoh did not want the Israelites to leave Egypt to go on a three-day journey in the desert and offer sacrifice to God. Could it be that the gods of Egypt knew that they would return, and this time not as slaves but as a mighty military that no one could defeat? Not even all the powers of the world united can fight against God's military. Their defeat is eminent, and we will see the triumph of the Immaculate Heart of Mary. This will be most humiliating to Satan and his legions, especially since our commander-in-chief is a woman.

Sure, there is the constant thirst in the desert, but we drink from the spiritual rock, which is Christ. We have the Eucharist instead of the manna, and we are called to live on every word that proceeds from the mouth of God. All we need is obedience to God, and the military campaigns will be successful.

Chapter X

Other Side of the Ocean

MY FLAME OF LOVE MUST BE CARRIED ACROSS TO THE OTHER SIDE OF THE OCEAN—THE RED SEA

THE FLAME OF LOVE BEING carried across to the other side of the ocean is symbolized as crossing the Red Sea to return to Egypt; not as slaves, but as warriors. Once again God will pass judgment on the gods of Egypt. The Hebrews are no longer slaves to Egyptians, and in modern history the Negroes are no longer slaves to Anglos; so what slavery is there to free people from? The simple truth is slavery to sin. But sin is the cause of our slavery, and the effect of sin is blindness. The battle we are fighting now is to free people from blindness. Jesus and Mary have made it clear that the only way to free slaves from blindness is to give sight to the slaves and to blind the slave owners—meaning the only way to free the oppressed is to blind the oppressors. The means of oppression in the world today is no different than it was during the time that the Israelites were slaves in Egypt. It is summed up in Pharaoh's statement: *"Look how numerous and* powerful the Israelite people are growing, more so than we ourselves! Come, let us deal shrewdly with them to stop their increase; otherwise, in time of war they too may join our enemies to fight against us, and so leave our country." Accordingly, taskmasters were set over the Israelites to oppress them with forced labor. (Exodus 1:9-11.) To put this in simple terms, "Let's oppress them with hard labor to limit their number of births." Pharaoh was concerned that the Israelites may leave Egypt. The question is, "How does oppression with hard labor limit the number of births of the oppressed?" In our times the answer to that question is that people believe that they cannot afford to have children. It is economic oppression to enforce population control. This oppression works against the kingdom of God. Since the Lord is the giver of life, it is safe to conclude that the oppressors have declared war on God. That's what modern day secularism is: a declaration of war against God.

To understand this paradox more deeply we must accept that there are spiritual realities that are not visible to the naked eye, such as: who were the gods of Egypt? The Lord would not waste time passing judgment on wooden statues, or even those made of gold. That would not accomplish anything. If we think of the mentality and ego that causes one to make a god, then we could possibly get closer to who these gods are. One reality is that the person who makes the image becomes the creator, and God becomes his creation. This is futile, and it is also the reason why his god or gods are called false gods. There is only one God, and He is Creator. Everything else is part of creation; visible and invisible. I guess it is nice to have a god that cannot tell you what to do, but it is still futile.

Another point of this reality is the caste system among

human beings. This goes against Scripture, which say that the Lord God made man in his image; male and female He made them. The caste system of superior and inferior humans is another declaration of war against God. Egyptians found the Hebrews abhorrent and would not sit at the same table with them. Also, does Anglo reference from heaven and Negro from the earth? If so, Anglos means angels—and yes, angels are superior to humans. Some are cast down to earth, and some are raised up from the earth. The child in the womb is being raised up from the earth, as the Lord God formed the first man. Those from above are trying to prevent these children of God from being born. They do not want the Lord God to breathe into the nostrils of these children the breath of life, and they become living beings. The legalized segregation of the child in the womb from those already born makes real in our time the story of Egypt. One thing all the oppressed have in common is the denial of citizenship. They are all orphans without a home. Remember how painful Elizabeth Kindelmann said that it was to hear this said about herself? No one wants to remain an alien their entire life, but that is what the caste system is all about.

So what should we do about this attack against the family? The Flame of Love movement increased its military by freeing souls from purgatory with the Monday fast and daily communion. Jesus said that each time we observe the Monday fast of bread and water, the soul of a priest would be set free from the place of suffering. Also each time we receive communion during that week, a multitude of souls would be set free from purgatory. I would suggest we follow Jesus' instructions for praying for the family. We may as well start with our own family; Jesus said this is our principle mission. Of utter importance is reparation, and Jesus gave request for this also. It looks like anyone looking to develop a prayer life and spirituality can benefit from using this model given by Jesus to Elizabeth Kindelmann. It would have to be adjusted to fit reasonably in each individual's state of life, and since it was given through private revelation, there are gifts awarded to those who heed the request. Jesus promised to award us in several ways and we know that He is trustworthy, because He is God. I'm suggesting that we put into practice the weekly agenda that Jesus gave to Elizabeth Kindelmann. It is the most effective form of military tactics imaginable. And, again I reiterate that all of this came to us through private revelation. That means no one is obligated to believe or practice this devotion. It also means that those who believe and practice the Flame of Love devotion may contribute in their own way whatever they are able. The weekly agenda is not a rule such as those lived out in religious orders. Individually, they are moreso requests of Jesus to accomplish certain advancements for the Kingdom of God. No one has to follow the weekly agenda fully the way that Elizabeth Kindelmann did—we are called to do whatever we can. We pray for this daily: "Thy kingdom come, thy will be done, on earth as it is in heaven." At this time in history we have a chance to help bring this into fulfillment, by participating in the ascetical practices of the weekly agenda.

    Back to limiting the increase of the people of God. Hard labor was not effective enough for Pharaoh, so he told the midwives when you see a Hebrew woman giving birth, if it is a boy kill him; but if it is a girl, she may live. That means that the child was killed during delivery, to prevent it from being born into the family—further proved by the midwives' response to Pharaoh about why his demand was not carried out. They said that the Hebrew women give birth before the midwife arrives—indicating that once the child was born, it was too late carry out Pharaoh's demand.

I would like to use the help of images to help demonstrate why it was too late after the child was born, and why Pharaoh took more drastic measures to accomplish his goals. The objective was to keep the boy from being born into the family. This is male and female coming together, with the family being female. For Christians, the family is the domestic church, and the church is always feminine; she is the bride of Christ.

Now take note of what Pharaoh does after his plan fails to stop the baby boys from being born into the family. He decides to kill *all* the baby boys that have been born. In our society it means after they have been conceived. It is the removal of the boy from the family, the same way the fetus is removed from the mother. I used the term "fetus" for greater clarity to non-believers, but it is actually a child.

One reason for desiring to limit the number of births among the people of God would be to impede the coming of the Kingdom of God as prayed in the Lord's Prayer.

Let's read what Jesus said to Elizabeth Kindelmann about this: *"What I am saying now is for you and all mothers who work according to My Heart. Your work is not of less value than that of persons raised to the highest priestly dignity. Mothers of families, you must understand your sublime vocation to populate My Kingdom and to fill the places left vacant by the fallen angels. Each step of My Holy Mother the Church starts from your heart* and your lap. My Kingdom grows inasmuch as you, mothers, nurture the created souls. You have the greatest work requiring a heightened sense of responsibility. Be fully aware that I have placed in your hands the task of leading a multitude of souls to eternal salvation."

During Holy Mass, He meditated with me on the words He had pronounced the previous year. And in the profound silence which filled my soul, with moving and kinds words, thus spoke the Lord Jesus:

Jesus: "I give you My special blessing for this work that carries such great responsibility. Through your spiritual director, send My petition to the Holy Father."

While I was writing, the Lord Jesus asked me to write these messages in red and to join them to the other ones.

Jesus: "Send My petition to the Holy Father because it is through him that I want to grant My blessing which carries great graces. At each opportunity, let them give a special blessing to those fathers who, in this great work of creation, collaborate with Me and accept My Holy Will. This unique blessing is reserved only for fathers. At the birth of each child, I pour out extraordinary graces on these families." (Spiritual Diary of Elizabeth Kindelmann, page 202.)

The statement about filling the places left vacant by the fallen angels seems revealing of why the fallen angels are trying to impede the coming of the kingdom. We pray for the coming of the kingdom in the Lord's Prayer, *"Thy Kingdom come, thy will be done, on earth as it is in heaven."* However, in the gospels, when the demons acknowledge that they know who Jesus is, they asked Jesus, "Have you come to torment us before it is time?" It appears they have good reason to impede the coming of the kingdom.

Of course, the main reason for killing all the baby boys in Egypt was to prevent one person from being born. It was to stop Moses from being born because he would lead the Israelites out of slavery in Egypt. More importantly, Moses' story foreshadows Jesus' story where Herod had all of the baby boys in Jerusalem put to death to prevent the newborn King of the Jews from saving the world. He would lead us out of slavery to the devil.

On an apparently smaller scale, take notice that the artificial contraception debate became a big deal in the United States a short time preceding the birth of Martin Luther King Jr. He is a Moses-type figure to the Negroes, whereas Moses was sent to free the Hebrews. When artificial contraception failed to accomplish their goals, abortion was legalized, meaning assassination. Just in case he was not the one, or maybe there was another, the shotgun approach is applied. They are correct in believing that Martin Luther King Jr. was not alone; the other prophet was St. Pio of Pietrelcina. There are many more prophets of our time, all sent at a particular time for a particular purpose. But these two prophets allow us to view the Old Testament and New Testament stories simultaneously: Moses leading the Hebrews out of oppression, and Jesus taking on our suffering.

The reason that the Flame of Love will return to Egypt is for the salvation of souls. The whole pilgrimage is for the salvation of souls. When the Lord made Pharaoh's heart obstinate, it was to give glory to God. In that way, the Egyptians will remember the mighty deeds of the Lord and they can be saved also. So the Flame of Love Pilgrimage through Egypt will cause Satan to be blinded, and the Lord will pass judgment on the gods of Egypt. The three days of darkness came before the death of the firstborns of Egypt. But the main objective of all of this, is the salvation of souls. Everything is done for this purpose. Egypt will be resurrected once the effusion of grace of the Flame of Love has taken place there.

Chapter XI

Those Signed with the Cross

ALL THE SOULS MARKED WITH THE SIGN OF THE BLESSED CROSS OF MY DIVINE SON—LOT AND FAMILY

WHEN THE FLAME OF LOVE reaches Sodom and Gomorrah, the outcome will be totally different from when Lot and his family left. The fire and brimstone destroyed lives and property in that place. The Flame of Love is a different type of fire. It is a soft gentle light that gives no cause for suspicion. It will unite the descendants of Lot and those of Abraham.

It will be as the day when Melchiezedec brought bread and wine for the sacrifice. On that day, the king of Sodom said to Abram, *"Give me the people; the goods you may keep"* (Genesis 14:221.) Abram wanted nothing from the king of Sodom, although he probably had the right to keep them as subjects since he had rescued them. Regardless, the people, including Lot, went back to Sodom. When the Flame of Love movement reaches Sodom, the families of Abraham and Lot will reunite. And once they begin to pray together, they will stay together.

The mission of the Flame of Love is to change hearts. The descendants of Abraham and Lot will realize that the land is able to support both groups. Of course the ancient cities of Sodom and Gomorrah were destroyed. When I speak of the Flame of Love movement reaching Sodom, I am speaking of a symbolic name for certain groups who are in need of being liberated.

In the Book of Revelation, a city is mentioned whose symbolic names are Sodom and Egypt. The journey from Egypt to Sodom is to bring the Flame of Love to the city that killed the prophets and their Lord, traditionally known as Jerusalem. Distinctly opposite of that city is Budapest. Although the Nazis and Communists tried to make Budapest like Sodom and Gomorrah, their efforts failed, thanks to the effusion of grace of the Flame of Love of the Immaculate Heart of Mary.

To reflect on the sins of Sodom, we may look at how the men of the city tried to overpower Lot, and demanded that he send his guests out so they can have relations with them. Lot was willing to do whatever it took to protect his guests. It is difficult to understand why Lot offered his daughters to these men in order to protect his guests, but this story has a deeper meaning than what is on the surface.

The story began with the Lord appearing to Abram as three men. Two of them went down to Sodom to see if the evil in Sodom was as bad as the reports the Lord had received. Both Abram and Lot recognized the time of their visitation. They would not let the Lord pass them by.

For us, the Most Holy Trinity dwells within our souls, but for them the Lord visited their homes. We live in the period of sanctification, and the work of this period belongs to the Holy Spirit. So when the Blessed Virgin revealed that the Flame of Love from her Immaculate Heart is her Son Jesus Christ, it means that we are living in a special time of grace. At this time in salvation history the Holy Spirit sanctifies, and the light of Christ blinds Satan. We have been given a preview of how this works: the Lord enlightened Lot and his family, but blinded the men of Sodom.

    The Angel of the Lord instructed Lot and his family to run to the hills and not look back, but Lot's wife looked back and turned into a pillar of salt. More symbolism implied here; we are the salt of the earth, so Lot's wife is preserving something valuable. If the pillar has four sides, it would mean she represents four churches, better known by the names of four cities. They have been preserved in time and waiting to be redeemed by the Flame of Love of the Immaculate Heart of Mary, which is Jesus Christ himself.

    Lot's daughters plotted a scheme to get him drunk and lie with him in order to have offspring with their father. The first night the older daughter went in and lay with him, and the next night the younger daughter went in and lay with him. Lot, however was not aware of his daughters lying down or getting up. Thus both of Lot's daughters became pregnant by their father. The older daughter conceived and gave birth to a son whom she named Moab, saying, "From my father." He is the ancestor of the Moabites of today. The younger daughter gave birth to a son and she named him Ammon, saying, "The son of my kin." He is the ancestor of the Ammonites of today.

    Sodom represents impurity and the destruction of marriage and family. The illicit relations between Lot and his daughters have kept alive the memory of Sodom and Gomorrah. The names Moab and Ammon automatically cause one to reflect on the story of Sodom and Gomorrah. The Flame of Love has gone forth from Buda and Pest destined to reach Moab and Ammon. Hopefully they will recognize the time of their visitation, as Lot did. The Lord must be welcomed into their homes. The people themselves must become living tabernacles in which the Lord Jesus dwells.

The Flame of Love movement, gone out from the four churches in the capital city of Budapest, must reach Lot's wife, the four churches that have been preserved. These four churches are waiting to be liberated. The movement is also destined to liberate Lot's descendants, the two kingdoms, that were newly established.

We live in a time in which it is considered immoral to use expressions such as sexual perversion. It is difficult to convince even Christians that sexual relationships outside of the marriage of a man and a woman are illicit. Society today believes that any relationship between consenting adults is appropriate and should receive the blessing of the church. What was once an abomination and called for the death penalty by God, is now defined by society as the will of God and has His blessing. What was good in the past is now looked upon as evil, and what was evil is now called good. When political leaders pass unjust and immoral laws, the people are scandalized. They are led into sin by those in authority, in the same way that children can be led into sin by adults.

Sodom is like Egypt. They have both declared war against God. Egypt declared war by legalizing artificial contraception, abortion and euthanasia. Sodom has declared war against the Almighty God by trying to redefine marriage. Many Christian denominations have accepted these practices that were once considered evil. A few decades ago not one denomination accepted artificial contraception or abortion. The Catholic Church remains firm in its understanding of faith and morals, but many of its members do not accept the teaching authority of the church. This problem is huge; the world is in grave danger. Christians have taken their stand and their battle cry is, "We have no king but Caesar." Our only hope is a change of heart within every individual. When enough people have been enlightened with the Spirit of Truth, Satan will be blinded by the light of Christ, and the world will know peace as never before.

May our feet journey together,
May our hands gather in unity,
May our hearts beat in unison,
May our souls be in harmony.

Chapter XII

Even the Non-Baptized

THE EFFUSION OF GRACES WILL ALSO REACH THE SOULS OF THE NON-BAPTIZED—THE FLOOD

THE BLESSED VIRGIN MARY SAID to Elizabeth Kindelmann: "*The Flame will ignite and will reach the whole world, not only in the nations consecrated to me, but all over the earth. It will spread out even in the most inaccessible places, because there is no place inaccessible to Satan. From it, draw strength and confidence. I will support your work with miracles as never seen before, and that the reparation to my Divine Son will accomplish imperceptibly, gently and silently.*" (Spiritual Diary of Elizabeth Kindelmann, page 61.)

The Flame of Love movement is a pilgrimage which began in the upper room. It is a new Pentecost, and the first ones to receive and spread the Flame of Love were those living in the house of the Carmelite fathers. This pilgrimage started where the Old Testament pilgrimage ended. In this book, we have journeyed from this new Pentecost back to the flood of Noah's time;

the flood that covered the entire earth and only eight people survived.

To understand better the cause of the flood, let's reflect on these passages from sacred Scripture.

Origin of the Nephilim. *1 When men began to multiply on earth and daughters were born to them, 2 the sons of heaven saw how beautiful the daughters of man were, and so they took for their wives as many of them as they chose. 3 Then the LORD said: "My spirit shall not remain in man forever, since he is but flesh. His days shall comprise one hundred and twenty years."*

4 At that time the Nephilim appeared on earth (as well as later), after the sons of heaven had intercourse with the daughters of man, who bore them sons. They were the heroes of old, the men of renown.

Warning of the flood. *5 When the LORD saw how great was man's wickedness on earth, and how no desire that his heart conceived was ever anything but evil, 6 he regretted that he had made man on the earth, and his heart was grieved.*

7 So the LORD said: "I will wipe out from the earth the men whom I have created, and not only the men, but also the beasts and the creeping things and the birds of the air, for I am sorry that I made them." But Noah found favor with the LORD.

11 In the eyes of God the earth was corrupt and full of lawlessness. 12 When God saw how corrupt the earth had become, since all mortals led depraved lives on earth, 13 he said to Noah: "I have decided to put an end to all mortals on earth; the earth is full of lawlessness because of them. So I will destroy them and all life on earth." (Genesis 6:1-7,11-13.)

After the flood, God established a covenant with Noah and his sons: *"I will establish my covenant with you, that never again* shall all bodily creatures be destroyed by the waters of a flood; there shall not be another flood to devastate the earth." (Genesis 9:11.)

The apparent connection between Egypt and our times is about procreation or sexual reproduction. Christians must learn to never give the devil an inch, because if we do he will take a mile. The child in the womb is deprived of the right to life. The liberal block calls this "reproductive rights," and they fight hard for the rights of women. At any given time, this so-called "right" can be transferred by lawmakers to the government. When this happens, women will lose their reproductive rights and will be in the same predicament as the child in the womb. If this so-called "reproductive right" is transferred to the government, there will be forced abortions and euthanasia. If anyone thinks this is farfetched, look at the Communist countries. This already exists, because they are atheist. We however are only halfway towards atheism. The child in the womb has lost its rights, but the mother still has hers—halfway meaning the devil has only been given an inch. We will become fully atheistic once the devil takes a mile; then women will lose their reproductive rights. We must fight tirelessly to prevent this from happening. At the same time, we must break free from the caste system of paganism, and assure that everyone has the right to life, liberty and the pursuit of happiness. The Flame of Love can help. Everyone who loves desires life, liberty and the pursuit of happiness for their loved ones.

The sins of Sodom and Gomorrah were evidently not considered sins by the citizens of those cities. The destruction of the institution of marriage signals the breakdown of a society. Those who are in opposition to God and church may see this as the destruction of the domestic church; if so, they are correct. The best way to destroy a structure is to destroy its foundation, but the family is also the foundation of secular societies. This behavior is self-destructive. The Flame of Love can help. Jesus said about the Most Holy Virgin: *By her powerful intercession, she obtained from Me for families this great effusion of grace, which she also wants to extend to the whole world.*

Going from heart to heart, she places in your hands the Flame of Love of her heart. Through your prayers and sacrifices, it will blind Satan who wants to rule over families. (Spiritual Diary of Elizabeth Kindelmann, page 187.)

The last epic battle is the fight against corruption and lawlessness that exists today. How do we protect law-abiding citizens from those who live depraved lives? Theft and murder; these are the words that define a lawless part of society. There are many other crimes being committed, but theft and murder define the behavioral pattern of those who take from others whatever they cannot afford. Many people wonder how we got to the place where a person kills another and steals his car, only because he needed a ride across town, or he needed a getaway car to commit a robbery. The crimes are many and the list would be too long if we tried to list them here. The concern of many citizens is what should be done about this seemingly hopeless situation. The first thing is to realize that the situation is not hopeless, but that the perpetrators of these crimes are people without hope. Jesus told Elizabeth Kindelmann that when people lose hope they are ready to commit sin. The reason they are without hope is because they have been deprived of the truth.

This lawlessness began in heaven. When the sons of heaven took the daughters of man, they began to form a society that would lose faith, hope and charity. It may take a long time—maybe centuries—but eventually there will be a caste system that oppresses a certain group. Once this group loses hope, they are ready to commit sin. I would like to clarify that when I say "lose hope," I mean specifically hope in God. The virtues of faith, hope and charity can be lost in a society or part of society that becomes convinced that it is impossible to know the truth.

The story of the sons of heaven taking as wives the daughters of man is about the fallen angels establishing a system of every imaginable false religion. It is understood that the intercourse is not sexual, because angels are pure spirits. But just like the church is the bride of Christ, these groups of people are considered brides of the sons of heaven. It started with one woman and one angel; Eve and the serpent. By the time of the flood, only God knows how many of the fallen angels had established a dwelling. The intercourse is conversation, such as the conversation between Eve and the serpent. The climax of the conversation is when she conceived the lie. The firstborn is a giant. In reality, Adam and Cain are giants and their renown exists even today. Cain is a giant, known as a liar and a murderer much like the serpent, who is the father of lies, and the author of death.

Those deprived of the truth will become liars and murderers, as we see today. It seems hopeless, but there is always hope for those who have faith in God. Our hope is reparation to Jesus in the Blessed Sacrament and to His Sacred Passion. These are the Thursday and Friday devotions that Jesus gave to Elizabeth Kindelmann in the weekly agenda. The Blessed Virgin told Elizabeth: *"I will support your work with miracles as never seen before, and that the reparation to my Divine Son will accomplish imperceptibly, gently and silently."*

"My little one, I extend the effect of grace of the Flame of Love of my heart over all the peoples and nations, not only over those living in the Holy Mother Church, but over all the souls marked with the sign of the blessed Cross of my Divine Son. Also over those who are not baptized!" (Spiritual Diary of Elizabeth Kindelmann, page 298.)

You have to seek a refuge for my Flame of Love, which is Jesus Christ himself. (Spiritual Diary of Elizabeth Kindelmann, page 78.)

While the Blessed Virgin was speaking about the Carmel, Jesus interrupted: "Because the Flame of Love of the heart of My Mother is Noah's Ark." (Spiritual Diary of Elizabeth Kindelmann, page 294.)

The Blessed Virgin encouraged me again. Mary: "Tell those who have responsibility not to be afraid and to trust me. I will protect them under my motherly mantle. Let the eight best-attended sanctuaries in the country and four churches dedicated to me in the capital city begin simultaneously this devotion, the handing over of my Flame of Love. Ardently long to make sacrifices, my little Carmelite. Constantly feed the Flame of my Love by your sufferings." (Spiritual Diary of Elizabeth Kindelmann, page 34.)

The Flame of Love will go out from the eight best-attended sanctuaries in the country of Hungary, just as eight people went out from Noah's ark to repopulate the earth after the flood. They will go out seeking a refuge for the Flame of Love, which is Jesus Christ Himself. God has blessed them and given instructions to: "Be fertile and multiply and fill the earth"—reaching those who are not baptized by blinding Satan, and setting them free from bondage. As this occurs, the four churches dedicated to the Blessed Virgin in the capital city of Budapest will spread the Flame of Love among Christians. We do not go out of the ark when we spread the Flame of Love; those who receive the Flame of Love are brought into the ark.

Flame of Love devotees: people of faith, hope and charity. Our hope is found in the words of our Lord Jesus and our Blessed Mother. If we do not offer reparation for the lawless, we render them hopeless and helpless. We must do all we can to get these poor sinners into the ark, and save the lives of as many as possible, even those who would have been murdered by the lawless. The Flame of Love must spread over the entire earth as the flood of Noah's time did. This is what our Lord Jesus and our Blessed Mother desire. Once the entire earth has experienced the Spirit of Love flooding the earth with its power, the earth will know peace, and the children of God shall witness and rejoice in the triumph of the Immaculate Heart of Mary.

May our thoughts be as one,
May our ears listen to the silence together,
May our glances profoundly penetrate each other,
May our lips pray together to gain mercy from the Eternal Father.

www.ingramcontent.com/pod-product-compliance
Lightning Source LLC
Chambersburg PA
CBHW050443010526
44118CB00013B/1660